Cyclist in You

A 28 Day Shift

By

JON PAUL TUCKER

Table of Contents

Forward

The bicycle, as both a vehicle and a metaphor, has always enabled me to explore new places, interact with my surroundings in new ways and open my eyes to new ways of seeing things. As one who loves to merge my devotion to Christ with my passion for the bike, I am always seeking ways to transfer my love of both to everyone I meet. In this book, Jon has very adeptly used cycling terminology, imagery and stories to share these passions.

I first became aware of Jon, and his unique perspective, a couple of years ago while I was serving as Christian Cycling President. Jon would submit poems and stories about his spiritual and cycling journeys for publication on our website. His stories were colorful, entertaining, inspiring, and at times exposed his vulnerability. It is easy to relate to his works, since much of what he writes about is as familiar as your favorite ride, but he always adds a twist of some sort from which we can learn, grow and blossom.

This easy-to-read text is something that I have been searching for years, a daily reflection that is encouraging, spiritual and growth promoting, written in a language that I, as a cyclist, know and love. Whether it's been years since you've thrown a leg over a top tube or you are a seasoned Category 1 racer, Jon's style will put you at ease while the content will stretch you and help you grow. It is as though you are in a paceline, sitting on Jon's wheel. You are cruising along comfortably behind him, but going faster and more efficiently than you could on your own, and enjoying every minute.

Tim Turnquist
Grassroots Initiatives Advocate at Venture.org
and Former Christian Cycling President

Introduction

E very one of us is a cyclist at heart, whether we realize it or not. Life is a series of cycles that we experience every day. My personal realization is that my life revolves around a 28-day cycle. In my world, this 28-day cycle is called shift work. I change from days to nights every 28 days. It takes a shift in your mindset to adjust to a schedule like this, especially if you are used to the cycle that most of the working world lives in, the five to six day cycle, which revolves around the 40 to 60 hour week.

Even if you don't do shift work, you go through cycles of change that can affect you like night and day! If you think of your life as a series of cycles, you will find that you are always in one of three places: at the start of a cycle, in the middle of a cycle, or at the end of a cycle. Like me, you are a cyclist on your journey through life. How you pedal through life is important, and why you do it is the goal.

In this book we are going to face the challenges of the cyclist. Through preparation, inspiration and dedication, we are going to develop a successful mindset over a 28-day cycle. My five-step system will help you through the cycle of revolution: **Read, Ride, Record, Revolt and Repeat**. This cycle of revolution is the axis of change within you that will access change for you!

Whether you are an amateur or a professional cyclist, we all share the common denominator of going through cycles in our lives. If we find ourselves in a challenging life cycle, it might take a "revolution" to change it, a complete turnaround to overcome it and emerge victorious. At times, this revolution can seem impossible, no matter how strong we are. The grace of God is what can give us the strength to create change. "With God," the Bible says, not apart from God, "all things are possible." (*Matthew 19:26*) So keep cycling my friend, and may the grace and the peace of God be with you from now to eternity.

Quotable Quote

"Grace is the possibility of God in our life that changes us!"

Acknowledgements

W here do I begin and how do I give thanks to all the people who have helped me as I cycled through life? Learning to ride a bike had to be one of the most important things I learned as a kid, and at the time, I didn't even know it. Today it has taught me so much about myself and this wonderful thing we call life. My brothers, Tom and Stan, had the biggest influence on me in those younger days growing up on the hill. Thanks to them I encountered many bumps and bruises along the way, and I somehow managed to avoid broken bones!

It was my parents who gave me many opportunities in life, but the greatest was a loving Christian home. My three brothers and my sister helped steer my decisions many times. Our family has grown so much that I can hardly keep up these days. There are so many nieces and nephews, even great nieces and great nephews, all of whom have played a part in my life. That family also includes my in-laws, who have made a huge impact on my journey through life. I am so thankful for my wife's side of the family, as they have taught me many irreplaceable life skills.

I can't forget my elementary and high school teachers, who had a voice in my life and challenged my thinking and my writing skills. If only I had listened more! Thankfully, I did learn how to type, thanks to Mrs. Atwell. White-out was the spell check of that day. And then there were the coaches. Coaches for baseball in the summer, football in the fall, and of course my favorite, basketball. I was so thankful to Coach Wells, who helped me with the fundamentals of shooting the jump shot, and Coach Daniels, who told me to "Play like it is Sunday afternoon."

My close friends are few and far between, but their value to my life cannot be replaced. Every time I hear their voices, the past and the present collide, and it is as if we never missed a beat. They never grow old to me, even though the signs that we are aging are evident.

I can't forget to mention my coworkers, who over the years jabbed at me and made my life at work so much fun. These last few years have been fun, and I have enjoyed the laughs! Thanks to those coworkers who took the challenge to ride and became fit and better as individuals.

The highlight of my life is, of course, my lovely wife Brenda of 30 years. Without her, I have no idea where my life would have led me. And I cannot fail to mention Gabrielle, my beautiful 16 year-old. She brings such joy to our lives. These two ladies complete me in so many ways.

Thanks to my publisher and editors and all those who encouraged me as I was writing this book. It has had its own revolutionary effect on me. By the time this is published, I will be 50. With this book, I take ownership of my past and say farewell, the present I embrace with confidence, and to the future I look ahead with eyes of faith and see hope!

Finally, thank you Lord for your great love, compassion and grace. You have shown me the fullness of life, the joy of living, and you have given me the faith to receive it. Without you I am incomplete and completely undone.

Jon Paul Tucker

Revolutions 2016

Putting a positive spin on Life!
Learning is winning, while cycling and spinning,
2015 was only the beginning.
A new year has begun, new cycles to be spun,
My core is complete in Christ the Son,
So when I am finished He'll say 'Well done.'

Five success steps I have learned,
In 'life cycles' as they've turned.
It starts with Reading so I can grow,
Riding my bike to get in the flow,
Recording my miles and setting my goals,
Revolting for change is how I roll.
Repeating these steps for 28 days,
Finding success in five easy ways.

Five essentials to nurture each day,
My faith comes first to point the way,
My family stands out as central to me,
My fitness to witness for all to see,
My finances a gift a treasure to share,
My future is bright with the dreams it bears.

These are my New Year's Resolutions,
For 2016 is 'The Year of Revolutions!'

By Jon P. Tucker
December 30, 2015

Week 1 – The Foundations of Fitness

Preparation

If you could see every struggle or challenge before it got to you, wouldn't you prepare yourself for it? In Oklahoma, when we see the clouds moving in from the southwest, we immediately turn on the television to check the weather, especially in the springtime. The truth is, the storms of life are going to come, so you might as well get ready. Jesus said, "In this world you will have trouble" (John 16:33) Today we have to prepare our mind for the upcoming 28-day challenge and learn how to use this book. I have taken it and broken it down into five easy–to-remember steps.

How to use this book

- **Read** - Read the daily topic and meditate on it.
- **Ride** - Get up and ride while you think about what you just read.
- **Record** - Write down your miles, notes and thoughts for the day's topic. Set a goal.
- **Revolt** - Revolt against the things you desire to change in your life and work towards goal.
- **Repeat** - Keep going and habits will form, and your mindset will change.

It's that simple! I believe that when you follow these five steps you will start to develop a habit that will change your mindset over the next 28 days.

Another thing I want to point out is that you can take this book and use it over a 31-day month, since we have seven of them in a calendar year. Use the chapter **Preparation** for Day 1, *Inspiration* for Day 16 and **Dedication** for Day 31. I've included a cycling log for these days as well. Also provided is a 31-day reading plan of proverbs for everyday wisdom.

Review and Reflect
- Read = daily: What was the main theme of today's topic?
- Ride = miles: How many miles did I ride?
- Record = notes: What did I learn today? Set a goal.
- Revolt = change: What changes do I need to work on to achieve my goal?
- Repeat = tomorrow: Consistency produces results!

Cycling Log

Bike/Type _____ Day _____ Month _____ Year _____

Weather: ☐ Sunny ☐ Cloudy ☐ Windy ☐ Rain ☐ Snow ☐ Other
Read: Topic of the day

_____

_____

Ride and Record

Miles _____ Route _____

Time _____ Average Speed _____

Revolt
Change, goals, thoughts of the day

_____

_____

_____

_____

_____

_____

• 31-day reading plan: Proverbs 1

5

Day 1 - Life Cycles

This is the topic that started the inspiration for this book. I realized that we all have something in common. Everybody goes through "stuff." You can put your own label on whatever you want to call your "stuff." For me, it isn't always the big stuff. It is the little stuff as well. And most of the time, if we just take care of the little stuff, the big stuff becomes a lot easier to deal with.

Every one of us is going through what I call life cycles. Our lives can be broken up into a series of cycles. Whether we find ourselves in a cycle of age, careers, finances, relationships, education, hobbies, health issues, death or even church, each cycle represents a cycle of change. The reality is that you will always find yourself in a part of a cycle, whether you are starting a cycle, right in the middle of a cycle or finishing a cycle.

If, for example, I look at the last 20 years of my life, technology alone has gone through many cycles of change. Do you ever remember talking so much about updates and apps in your life 20 years ago? Sure, you updated your car every four to six years or you updated your home every ten years, but today something in technology is being updated even as I type! My computer just displayed this message: "All changes saved to your drive." But let's slow down and take a look at our former years. Paul said, "When I was a child, I talked like a child, I thought like a child, I reasoned like a child. When I became a man, I put the ways of childhood behind me." (*1 Corinthians 13:11*) The transition from youth to adulthood represents a momentous cycle of change. With knowledge comes responsibility. We learn to take responsibility for what we know. Maturing into adulthood gives us the ability to respond to situations in an adult manner. I won't be using my training wheels to ride in a Gran Fondo[1]!

Today I am facing the fact that I will be turning 50 this coming year. It seems that all of my life has been in preparation for this moment, and yet this too will pass. But I intend to embrace it, enjoy it and hopefully celebrate my own Jubilee for this next life cycle I am about to enter. My vision is to still be riding into my 70s and to enjoy each life cycle while on my bicycle. And the way I plan to achieve this goal is to embrace it 28 days at a time.

So the question is: "Is your life cycling properly?" Or do you feel like you are stuck in a cycle that will not change? Remember that change is inevitable, but how you deal with it is your choice. Not all changes are bad. In fact, most changes are good! It would be very hard to go back to training wheels after 40 plus years of being free from them. But sometimes we need to retrain our thinking to break certain cycles we are in.

---

[1]   Gran Fondo is an Italian word that loosely translates as "Big Ride." It is a type of long distance road bicycle race in which riders are individually chip-timed. The first Gran Fondo was held in Italy in 1970; Gran Fondos have now become popular throughout North America, Australia and increasingly worldwide.

You can work the change or change can work you. That's the rub. So here is God's one-word solution to change: Grace! God's grace over the action in our lives breaks the cycle by changing the things inside that we alone cannot. It is called a "Revolution of Grace"! This revolution represents a complete turnaround, so that when you come back to where you started, you have changed. You can't bring about complete change through your work alone; it is His grace at work in you that helps change you! Through His grace you become more complete in change. Why do I believe grace is so important in helping us change? It is because grace cannot be earned. Once we have done all we can do, God compensates for our lack in grace.

You have to give up your seat in the saddle and stop cranking and let Him take over so that you end up where you need to go. The end result is better than the beginning because real change does that. Humility is the key to unlocking this principle of change in your life and mindset. Without humility you can be lost in selfish delusions. The Bible tells us to "humble ourselves before God" and reminds us that "pride goes before a fall." (*James 4:10, Proverbs 16:18*)

Review and Reflect
- Each and every one of us is going through stuff.
- Change is inevitable, but how you deal with it is your choice.
- Not all change is bad. Most change is good.
- God's grace in action breaks us out of cycles we are stuck in.
- Humility is the key to unlocking change in our lives and our mindset.

Quotable Quote

"Take action to embrace the cycle you are in before you are embarrassed by the cycle you are on!"

Cycling Log

Bike/Type _____ Day _____ Month _____ Year _____

Weather: ☐ Sunny ☐ Cloudy ☐ Windy ☐ Rain ☐ Snow ☐ Other

Read: Topic of the day

_____

_____

Ride and Record

Miles _____ Route _____

Time _____ Average Speed _____

Revolt

Change, goals, thoughts of the day

_____

_____

_____

_____

_____

_____

- 31-day reading plan: Proverbs 2

Day 2 - The Axis of Change

What is central to your life? The earth takes 365 days to orbit the sun. How many decisions did you have to make during that time? No matter how you break it down, you and I are constantly changing. So we need to examine the core of who we are, what we believe and the decisions we have to make. Let's face it: the decisions we make determine the directions we take. At some point, it all comes down to you and taking the responsibility for your decisions in life.

The axis of change is the central point from where change needs to start. The central point is within each of us. Dealing with the self is the starting point of change on any level. This axis deals with what you believe, who you are and the decisions you make. These three things will determine your ability to access change.

I believe this is the point where we all must begin in order to turn our cycling into success. I am referring to two different types of cycling, life cycles and biking. Life cycles are naturally a part of each of our lives, while biking or cycling is a lifestyle choice. Not all of us are born natural athletes, so cycling can pose a challenge.

And even though life cycles are a part of us, not all of them are easy to roll with. Some require extra effort.

For now, I ask that you focus on the life cycles you have been going through. Think about the past year first, and look for things that have changed in that time. What brought you to the decision to get this book and read it? Was it because you realized there was a part of you that you would like to change? Take a minute to figure that out and write it down. Now you have something to work with.

The axis of change begins at the core of who you are. Though I probably don't personally know you, you are going to learn a lot more about me as you read this book. Hopefully, this book will help you learn more about yourself. As you apply the principles in this book, you are going to access change that can turn your cycling into success!

Write down your five core values. Think about these five core values and how you relate to each one. What is lacking in any of the five that you can do something about? This will give you plenty to think about during your ride today. Don't be hasty in figuring out what these core values are, and understand that it is okay to refine them as you go along.

My top five core values are my faith, family, fitness, finances and future. These things are essential in my life. They all revolve around one thing: relationship. How I relate to each of these five values is important. Maybe my core values are similar to yours. Knowing your core values will be important for the road ahead.

Determining your five core values is the key to understanding who you are. Knowing your core values will help you understand the decisions that you make. Everything you do from this point on should be done with your five core values in mind. Healthy core values help you balance everything in your life, and how well you understand yourself will really help your cycling in life. Understanding your natural ability will also help you determine what your cycling goals are and where to start.

(*2 Corinthians 13:5, Jeremiah 17:10*)

Review and Reflect

- The axis of change is our core.
- Three parts: Who you are, what you believe and decisions you make.
- Write down your top five core values.
- Your core values all revolve around relationship.

Quotable Quote

"To access change I need to understand the axis of change."

Cycling Log

Bike/Type _____ Day _____ Month _____ Year _____

Weather: ☐ Sunny ☐ Cloudy ☐ Windy ☐ Rain ☐ Snow ☐ Other

Read: Topic of the day

_____

_____

Ride and Record

Miles _____ Route _____

Time _____ Average Speed _____

Revolt

Change, goals, thoughts of the day

_____

_____

_____

_____

_____

_____

- 31-day reading plan: Proverbs 3

Day 3 - The Five Steps of Revolutions

There are five essential steps you need to take in order for your revolution to become a reality. A great way to help remember the steps is to use the fingers of your hand.

1. **Read: Build your mind.** Use your index finger to point the way, because this is the starting point.
2. **Ride: Build your body.** This step stands out the most, like your middle finger.
3. **Record: Build your spirit.** Write down your dreams, visions and goals. Be married to them as though they are the vows you took when you put a wedding band on your ring finger.
4. **Revolt: Build your change.** No matter what it is, it's often the small things that can make the biggest difference, so this step is represented by your pinky finger.
5. **Repeat: Build repetition.** This step helps you keep a good grip on what you are achieving. Without our opposable thumbs, we wouldn't be able to hold onto anything, so this step is represented by your thumb.

Now look at your hand and repeat these five steps of revolutions: Read, Ride, Record, Revolt and Repeat. With these five things at work in your life, you will see amazing results begin to take place as you practice them. Over the next 28-day cycle, and throughout the year, you can use this system of revolution to create real and lasting change. This is a lot like the age-old foundation of education reading, writing and arithmetic. When we read we learn, when we write we can see our goals, and when we do the math we can figure out the solutions to our problems.

Let's go over each step a little further.

Read – Build Your Mind

When we read, we build our mind by engaging it to learn. As you read this book, try not to hurry through it. Let it soak in. Continue this practice throughout the day and add other readings along the way that motivate you.

Ride – Build Your Body

This next step is fun because you get to get out and ride to build your body. This is when you can get your cardio going and process some of the material you have been reading. The great thing about the ride is that you can engage your whole being: spirit, soul and body. Often while I'm riding I pray and meditate on things I need to do and accomplish for that day. Some days this may be your starting point, and other days it may be the last thing you get to do. You may even have to work it into your lunch break. Whenever you do get to do this, make it great!

Record – Build Your Spirit

This step can build your spirit and your soul. Over time, you will find this becoming an important part of you because you will begin to see and define things in your life. You can capture your dreams, write a vision for that dream and then begin to set the goals you need to reach to get you there. That's what I love about this step. It is far more than just writing down miles. You can make it your time to write a to-do-list or revise the one you have. Make some vows, strong and willful commitments, and start living them out so that you will find success that brings inner peace.

Revolt – Build Your Change

Once you reach this step, if you have really stopped and listened to your heart, this one won't be that difficult to figure out. If you have taken those first three steps, the revolution will already be happening. At this point you will be ready to tackle your change! Realize that it may take some thought at first and even continued revolt, but if you stay committed, you will achieve the change you desire.

Repeat – Build Repetition

Repeat what you have done to help build repetition in your life. This will ensure that change is as constant as you need it to be. When you sow good habits, you reap good habits, so keep sowing into your success. The rewards will outweigh the heartache of what you are trying to change. In the end, you will also create a reputation within, and this reputation will be visible on the outside as well.

This five-step process of revolution is vital to your change, so don't change anything about it until you have learned it and know it like the back of your hand! Then you can use the process of revolutions to build your own blueprint for success in life.

(Mark 12:30, James 1:17)

Review and Reflect
• Read - Build your mind
• Ride - Build your body
• Record - Build your spirit
• Revolt - Build your change
• Repeat - Building repetition creates reputation

17

Quotable Quote

"When we read we learn, when we write we can see our goals and when we do the math we can figure out the solutions to our problems."

Cycling Log

Bike/Type _____ Day _____ Month _____ Year _____

Weather: ☐ Sunny ☐ Cloudy ☐ Windy ☐ Rain ☐ Snow ☐ Other

Read: Topic of the day

_____

_____

Ride and Record

Miles _____ Route _____

Time _____ Average Speed _____

Revolt

Change, goals, thoughts of the day

_____

_____

_____

_____

_____

_____

• 31-day reading plan: Proverbs 4

19

Day 4 - The Five Safeguards for Cycling

To withstand the test of time, a house must be built on a strong foundation. The same applies to cycling: there are fundamentals that we need to build on, whether we are riding for leisure, fitness, racing or just pure fun. So when I start out on a ride, I think first about the most important thing: my safety. Keeping safe should always be at the top of the list. Safeguards will help secure our foundation.

My Cycling Checklist
- Always wear a helmet. If you put this into practice every time you ride, it will soon become second nature. If I can feel my hair blowing in the wind, (what's left of it) I stop because I know I've forgotten something.
- Always wear gloves to protect your hands. The first time I went down a couple of years ago, I was so thankful I had gloves on.

Padded gloves help with grip and fatigue. For me, gloves are as important to safety as a helmet.

- Always wear glasses to protect your eyes from flying objects and UV sunrays. Your vision is important when you are riding and in every area of your life. "Where there is no vision the people perish." (*Proverbs 29:18*)
- Always dress appropriately. Is it going to rain? Is it hot? Is it cold? Dress for the weather.
- Always carry a few basic items that will help in an emergency. My list includes:
  - Water: Hydration is important for your ride.
  - Phone: You will need a cell phone in case of an emergency.
  - Inner tubes: Eventually, you will get a flat tire.
  - Tools: Air pump or cartridges, tire tools, multi wrench.
  - Lights: For safety in the early morning or evening hours, at the front and the back.
- Plan your route. Decide your route depending on the time of day. Ask yourself a few simple questions:
  - How is the weather going to affect my ride?
  - Am I wearing the right gear for the weather?
  - What is the traffic going to be like on the route I want to ride?
  - Will the sun be at my back or in my face?
  - Have I let anyone know where I am going to be riding?
  - Will I have cell phone service in the area?

All of these questions are important to your safety and should be considered. If you follow this foundational guide, I believe you will have a safe and successful ride.
(*Proverbs 2:11, John 15:17, Psalms 32:7*)

Review and Reflect

- Always wear your safety gear.
- Always dress for the weather.
- Always carry basic equipment to help you in case of an emergency.
- Always plan your route.
- Always make sure you have good communication on your route.

Quotable Quote

"Those who disregard safety place little value on their life or the lives of others."

Cycling Log

Bike/Type _____ Day _____ Month _____ Year _____

Weather: ☐ Sunny ☐ Cloudy ☐ Windy ☐ Rain ☐ Snow ☐ Other

Read: Topic of the day

_____

_____

Ride and Record

Miles _____ Route _____

Time _____ Average Speed _____

Revolt

Change, goals, thoughts of the day

_____

_____

_____

_____

_____

- 31-day reading plan: Proverbs 5

Day 5 - Five Life Essentials

The focus of Week One is: "Why do I ride?" This will continue to be our focus. It is important to establish your core values. Once you have figured out your core values, protecting them becomes vital. These core values are the foundation of life, fitness and cycling. This is what I have defined as the five essentials, or the big five "F" words to focus on:

* Faith: What you believe.
* Family: Who you are and where you came from.
* Fitness: What you do.
* Finance: What you earn.
* Future: Where you are going.

All of us are affected by these five essentials in some way, and all of them affect each other. I would like to break down the word FITNESS to get a handle on this and what it stands for to me.

25

- Faith
- Intellect
- Together
- Nurturing
- Essentials
- Sustains
- Success

Faith Intellect Together Nurturing Essentials Sustain Success

This is true fitness to me and defines why we do the things we do in life. Each of these elements has an effect on us. If you love your, family you will want to be healthy to enjoy them. If you stay fit, you can earn money to take care of your family. If you want to have a great future, taking care of your finances and health matters. And if you have faith, then all of these things will be possible, and you can sustain them and find success. These essentials are the links in the chain of your life that have to be oiled, maintained or nurtured regularly.

I would once again like to use the fingers on our hand to help us remember these five essential things:

- Faith is your index finger, to guide your way.
- Family is your middle finger because it stands out the most.
- Fitness is like the ring on your ring finger. It represents a lifelong commitment to maintaining good health.
- The financial aspect is like your pinky finger: taking care of the small things can create larger things in your life.
- Your future is like your thumb: without a future you would not have a grip on your life's goals and vision.

Another way to look at this is to understand that fitness is a seven letter word, and the number seven represents perfection. It represents the completion of the seven-day cycle, otherwise known as a week. If we break down the word fitness, the letter N separates the word FIT from the ESS in ESSentials. It is essential to keep nurturing the important things in your life. The word essentials is the longest of the seven words. Why is that? Because life is full of challenges. I have heard that five represents the number of grace. Both faith and grace are five letter words, and together I believe these will help you protect the essentials in your life every day. So stay fit and remain focused on the road ahead, and keep pedaling my friend!

(*Psalms 91*)

Review and Reflect

* The Big Question: "Why do I ride?"
* The five essentials are the five "F" words: Faith, Family, Fitness, Finance and Future.
* Nurture regularly.
* Protect your essentials.

Quotable Quote

*"I ride for the pleasure of recreation,
the purpose of fitness and for the love of my family."*

Cycling Log

Bike/Type _____ Day _____ Month _____ Year _____

Weather: ☐ Sunny ☐ Cloudy ☐ Windy ☐ Rain ☐ Snow ☐ Other

Read: Topic of the day

_____

_____

Ride and Record

Miles _____ Route _____

Time _____ Average Speed _____

Revolt

Change, goals, thoughts of the day

_____

_____

_____

_____

_____

- 31-day reading plan: Proverbs 6

Day 6 - Fall in Love Again

I t's the first day of fall 2015, and once again I am reminded of why I love to ride! Even though this one is starting off with above normal temperatures, I can feel the change in the air. The sun is setting earlier, and the mornings are much cooler. Great days for cycling!

So the question is, "Why do I love to ride?" The answer is pretty simple: recreational fitness. I want to live a long, healthy life and enjoy my days here on earth, and riding can help me achieve that goal. Besides, riding is fun! I can map out a route or just let the road lead me where it will. But the most important thing is learning that love takes work. You only get out of it what you're willing to put into it.

Along the way, I get to talk to people from all over about our common bond, cycling. This reminds me of the day that I got to ride with a fellow employee for the first time. So not only do I love to ride, I love having friends to enjoy the ride with. Friendship is important, both on and off the road. There is nothing better than a great ride with friends, family or the love of your life. After all, if fitness is a part of your goal, you might as well enjoy it with the ones you love.

Nearly 30 years ago, I fell in love with the woman who would become my wife. Sixteen years ago, we had our daughter, and ten years ago I decided I needed to be healthy and fit so I could take care of them in the long run. I also wanted to get fit enough to participate in a Gran Fondo. It started with running, and then I started biking for cross training and because it was easier on the joints. It was cycling that helped me create a lifestyle change.

I have two questions for you:

• Who is your first love?
• Are you ready to fall in love all over again?

Whether you are an avid cyclist or you just ride around the block once in a while, you might need a little reminder. Take a piece of paper out and write across the top "I love to ride because _____" and fill in the blank. Maybe you have one reason. Maybe you have a long list.

Here are a few more of the reasons that I love riding. Cycling relieves stress and is a great way to get some down time from work, whether it's going out on a weekend bike ride with a local cycling group or a few friends or riding around town with loved ones. It's a great feeling to compete in a race, to challenge yourself. Whatever the reason, fall in love again! You will be glad you did!

So let's apply this same principle to our relationship with Christ. Why did I fall in love with Him in the first place? This one is easy because the Bible answers this one for us. "We love Him because He first loved us." (*1 John 4;19*) But the real question is: "Has your love grown cold?" Again the Bible points us back to Him and calls us to "return to our first love." (*Book of Revelation 2:2-4*). We are reminded of our reason to love Him: ". . . we love him because he first loved us." (*1 John 4:19*) And that is the essence of today's devotional words, fall in love again. Fall in love again, not only with cycling but with your Lord and Savior Jesus Christ! Because *John 15:5* tells us: "... apart from me you can do nothing." Now is a great time, tomorrow may not be, yesterday is just a memory. So what are you waiting for? He is ready for whatever ride you want to take Him on. He will never leave you or forsake you.

(*Hebrews 13:5*)

Review and Reflect
* I love to ride because _____.
* Return to your first love.
* Apart from Him you can do nothing.
* He will never leave you or forsake you.

Quotable Quote

"The only time a fall is good is when the cause is love."

Cycling Log

Bike/Type _____ Day _____ Month _____ Year _____

Weather: ☐ Sunny ☐ Cloudy ☐ Windy ☐ Rain ☐ Snow ☐ Other

Read: Topic of the day

_____

_____

Ride and Record

Miles _____ Route _____

Time _____ Average Speed _____

Revolt

Change, goals, thoughts of the day

_____

_____

_____

_____

_____

- 31-day reading plan: Proverbs 7

Day 7 - The Rest Cycle

R est is an important part of living and is mentioned right at the beginning of the Bible. The pattern of rest was established by God himself. "By the seventh day God had finished the work he had been doing; so on the seventh day he rested from all his work." (*Genesis 2:2*)

So what about you? Are you getting enough rest in your life? If you are at all like me and probably like most of us, the answer is no. Well at least it doesn't seem like it. I saw a great comic strip clip where a guy was riding in about a foot of snow as he passed his neighbors. The caption read: "Didn't anyone tell Jim it's okay to take a day off?" Been there! Done that!

It's okay to take a break from your bike. In fact, your family might appreciate it! Sometimes we have to stop and smell something besides our sweat! Take a break and reflect on dreams and goals and the people in your life, and remember that you will get to ride again another day. Enthusiasm can sometimes blind us from things that need our attention. We can get so wrapped up in our own little cycling world that we forget about the rest of the world spinning around us. For some of us, cycling is an escape from the world around us. But at some point, the wheels have to stop turning and we just need rest.

I believe in a rest that is far greater than sleep. It is a rest inside that keeps us going, even when physically we are not getting all the rest we need. Every week we need a day of rest, and I believe in the pattern that God set up for us. One day can truly revive our spirit, soul and body. This rest is a given, no matter who you are. The other rest I am referring to is found in the book of *Hebrews 4:10*. His rest. What do you mean you may ask?

The rest that God gives us through Jesus Christ is a rest from striving. We often get caught in the vicious cycle of striving to please God or to please others. It is a pointless effort. No one can earn salvation, and as the saying goes, "You can't please everyone." We have to find rest in the finished work of Christ. We have to allow His grace at work inside of us become the rest from meaningless work. We can only do what we can do and allow Him to take care of you rest. We cannot always control the outcome of the circumstances life presents us, but we can control how we react through our own decisions. Choose to rest in Him for what He has already done and continues to do in your life. Rest is something that we need to get into the habit of doing. Only then can we truly enjoy the benefits, even on those days that we don't get the physical rest we would really like to. If you choose rest, you will have the energy to take care of the essential things in your life.

(*Genesis 2:2, Matthew 11:29*)

Review and Reflect
- Everyone needs to rest. It's okay to miss a day of biking.
- Everyone needs a day of rest. Take one day off each week from work.
- Rest is a choice. Choose wisely.
- His rest has benefits. No more striving.
- Rest is essential.

Quotable Quote

*"True rest is knowing that everything
I need for salvation is already done in Christ!"*

Cycling Log

Bike/Type _____ Day _____ Month _____ Year _____
Weather: ☐ Sunny ☐ Cloudy ☐ Windy ☐ Rain ☐ Snow ☐ Other
Read: Topic of the day

_____

_____

Ride and Record

Miles _____ Route _____

Time _____ Average Speed _____

Revolt
Change, goals, thoughts of the day

_____

_____

_____

_____

_____

- 31-day reading plan: Proverbs 8

Week 2 – Plan the Route

Day 8 - Cyclist versus Bike Rider

Maybe this is a silly question or concept, but I was thinking about this the other day. At what point do you become a cyclist? Let's face it: you learn to ride a bike when you are little, and as they say, "It's just like riding a bike." You never forget how. Of course if it has been a while, your balance might be an issue, but for the most part you never forget. Biking is a great skill! I wonder if I could add it to my resume?

I'd like to explore this a little deeper. One definition I heard probably wraps it up the best: A cyclist is a person who rides his bike even when he or she doesn't have to.

I grew up with older siblings, and they taught me a lot of different skills. Some I still use every day. Riding a bike doesn't come naturally, and I had to learn the hard way, by falling! Yep. I fell many times. And just like learning to walk, I never stopped trying. Sometimes I landed on the handlebars. They had no grips and it felt like I had been impaled! I distinctly remember having several round red marks on my stomach from that experience. Eventually, I got the hang of it, and off I went.

Several years ago, I purchased a mountain bike so I could start cross training and recover from running. I wasn't running a whole lot or getting ready for the Boston Marathon. It was clear to me that I was out of shape and needed to take control over my physical fitness. But I remember how fun it was to cover a mile so quickly on a bike after taking so long to run one. Needless to say, I would go out for several miles at a time, and I could really get the old cardio going.

It wasn't until recently that I embarked on this journey of cycling. I never thought of myself as a cyclist. I just knew about bicycles and could ride them. And then a couple of years ago, I thought, "What separates bike riders from cyclists?" I concluded it was the ability to commute from one community to another, and if you're really good, come back! So that is what I did. The nearest community to me was about 10 miles away, so I set out to become a cyclist. After I did it, I felt great. I felt a sense of accomplishment and felt that I could truly call myself a cyclist.

Then I realized it was much more than that. Commuting to the next place was just the first step in becoming a cyclist. Cycling is a lifestyle that takes discipline. You mean I have to ride? Well you don't have to ride, but if you want to improve you have to put in the time. I believe time in the saddle is a good way to gauge if you are a true cyclist.

Let's apply this to our own life with this question: "At what point do I go from just being a believer to becoming a true follower of Christ?" The Bible tells us that: ". . . even the demons believe this and they tremble." (*James 2:19*) Believing in and knowing about Him really isn't enough, is it? What it really takes is faith in what He did for us so we can experience His grace and through discipline become a true follower of Jesus Christ. It is when we walk in love that the world will know we are His disciples. That is when they will say they have been with Jesus and call us Christians. It's good to have the knowledge of something, but it is better when you know how to apply it. Once you apply it, it becomes wisdom, and then it becomes a part of you.

The Bible asks us this question: "What can separate us from the love of God?" (*Romans 8:38-39*) The answer is nothing! Nothing or no "thing" can separate us from His great love! So get ready to become a real cyclist, or at least become a cyclist at heart, by becoming a true believer and follower of Jesus Christ! That is what can really change your life and your life cycle!

Colossians 3:12, Romans 13:14

Review and Reflect

- A true cyclist is a follower of Jesus Christ. A bike rider wants to lead.
- A true cyclist lives from his heart. A bike rider doesn't know how to live.
- A true cyclist knows the purpose of his ride. A bike rider thinks he knows how to ride.
- A true cyclist rides with discipline because he has a goal. A bike rider rides occasionally.
- A true cyclist counts the cost of every ride. A bike rider has no account.
- A true cyclist knows the rules of the road. A bike rider has no rules.

Quotable Quote

"The difference between true and false is knowing your identity."

Cycling Log

Bike/Type _____ Day _____ Month _____ Year _____
Weather: ☐ Sunny ☐ Cloudy ☐ Windy ☐ Rain ☐ Snow ☐ Other
Read: Topic of the day

_____

_____

Ride and Record

Miles _____ Route _____

Time _____ Average Speed _____

Revolt
Change, goals, thoughts of the day

_____

_____

_____

_____

_____

_____

- 31-day reading plan: Proverbs 9

Day 9 - Shift Leader

S taring at a five week calendar, planning for the changes ahead: that's what those of us do who work shift work. We plan ahead for vacation, holidays, overtime, and who is going to be gone when. For some the concept may be foreign, but for me, it's a way of life. 12-hour day shifts for a 28-day cycle and then 12-hour night shifts for another 28 day cycle. But in reality, I only work 14 of those 28 days, so the payoff is time off.

I never planned to end up at a job like this, but here I am, and in the midst of it, there He is. God, that is. It wasn't until I started this job that I discovered my new hobby of cycling. So for me, this job, this lifestyle, has all become a huge blessing in my life. In fact, it was an answer to my prayers.

As with most journeys, you don't know exactly where you will end up, you only hope the place is close enough to where you were intending to go in the first place. And of course you hope that you are not disappointed with the accommodations once you get there.

For me, this life cycle was a change I needed. I had worked independently for years as a carpenter and done all kinds of handy work. Over 25 years I had worked for a few companies, but I always managed to end up working for myself, usually out of the back of my truck.

But then things began to change, and I had had enough. It was time to "work for the man," so to speak. I was ready for a change, a "shift" in my life. Clock in, clock out and go home. It took some time before I landed this job, and for three years I was content.

And then an opportunity came along, and I felt I could contribute more to the company I was working for. Besides, they were paying me well for what I did, and I had no complaints about my job. A shift leader job opened up in my department. So I talked to my wife about it, of course, and she said it sounded good. I pulled up the job posting on a computer at work. A man passing by stopped, looked at me, and said, "Shift leader." He walked away. I smiled, laughed to myself, and then thought that was a word from God. That man had no idea I was applying for this position! I'd never really talked to this man; he didn't even work in my department. I hadn't told anyone what I was doing.

To make a long story short, a week later I got the job. I hadn't told anyone about what that co-worker had said to me, and I was hoping to bump into him and ask him why he'd said what he did. A few days later, I was walking down the main hall, and there he was, sitting at one of the computers. I stopped and looked at him and called him by name and said, "So tell me, what you said to me, what was that all about?"

He answered very calmly, "The Lord told me to tell you that."

And I replied "I thought so, but I wanted to make sure."

Then he said, "So you got the job, didn't you?"

"Yes I did."

And so it was. God was doing His work in the workplace, showing up where I was. It should have come as no surprise, but it's always nice when God confirms what you are doing. Being in the right place and doing the right thing with the right people.

The job does not so much define me for who I am but more importantly who God has made me to be on the inside. He made me a leader for change and put me in a place where I could bring about a shift. Is there a change ahead for you? Is there a shift getting ready to happen? Be open, be ready and be willing. Let God lead you to his provision. "If you are willing and obedient you will eat the good of the land." (*Isaiah 1:19*)

Review and Reflect

- I had no complaints and was content.
- Opportunity will come along.
- God is at work in the workplace.
- Be open, be ready and be willing.

Quotable Quote

"If you can't see or recognize God showing up at your workplace, you may need a new workplace."

Cycling Log

Bike/Type _____ Day _____ Month _____ Year _____

Weather: ☐ Sunny ☐ Cloudy ☐ Windy ☐ Rain ☐ Snow ☐ Other

Read: Topic of the day

_____

_____

Ride and Record

Miles _____ Route _____

Time _____ Average Speed _____

Revolt

Change, goals, thoughts of the day

_____

_____

_____

_____

_____

_____

- 31-day reading plan: Proverbs 10

Day 10 - Reflectors

They are on every new bike, tucked into the spokes of the front and back wheel. You never really notice them. But they serve you well when you're out on an evening ride and darkness sets before you expect it. And when darkness sets in, you are not thinking about the reflectors or whether or not they are working. You are just trying to get home.

But those two reflectors serve as a safeguard for those moments when we get caught in the darkness. The odd thing is that you don't know if they're working. You can't even really see them from your spot in the bike seat, and they don't make a sound. Then a light reflects off them and they look like glowing circles because your wheels are spinning so fast. You are no longer swallowed up by darkness.

Often our own vision is blocked from seeing God at work in our lives. We feel like we are pedaling, but there is no evidence that the wheels are turning. We don't see the reflectors tucked away in the spokes of life during the dark times. It's only after the light of God's word hits them that we see that God was moving us along the whole time.

Reflection is a key part of our faith because we walk (ride) by faith not by sight (*2 Corinthians 5:7*). It's when we reflect back on an event that we can see the hand of God and His fingerprints of grace. Grace is a great reflector. You can't see it, but you know it's there. The same is true when we can't see God at work in ourselves. Others still see His reflection in us.

Reflect on what God has done in your life. Wasn't God there all along? Once you realize He was always there, keep those reflectors in place. They will serve you well on the road of life and remind you of His presence in every circumstance!

"Reflect on what I am saying, for the Lord will give you insight into all this." (*2 Timothy 2:7*)

"For now we see only a reflection as in a mirror; then we shall see face to face. Now I know in part; then I shall know fully, even as I am fully known." (*1 Corinthians 13:12*)

Review and Reflect
- Darkness can no longer hide you.
- Reflection is a key part of our faith.
- Grace is a great reflector.
- Reflect on what God has done in your life.

Quotable Quote

"Reflection opens our eyes to see God's grace at work in our lives!"

Cycling Log

Bike/Type _____ Day _____ Month _____ Year _____

Weather: ☐ Sunny ☐ Cloudy ☐ Windy ☐ Rain ☐ Snow ☐ Other

Read: Topic of the day

_____

_____

Ride and Record

Miles _____ Route _____

Time _____ Average Speed _____

Revolt

Change, goals, thoughts of the day

_____

_____

_____

_____

_____

_____

- 31-day reading plan: Proverbs 11

49

Day 11 - The Cycle of Choice

There is a bicycle to fit every rider in the world! Millions of bicycles are produced worldwide each year. Like everything else in this world, each year a new and improved model comes out. Specialized, Giant and Trek, just to name a few of the brands we ride. Back in my day it was Schwinn that seemed to dominate the market. The good news about all this is that we have choices.

I love having choices in my life, especially when it comes to the things I enjoy. You mean I don't have to choose vanilla every time? How about a little ice cream mixed with a heath bar in an oversized waffle cone? How easily we can get distracted by too many choices! You can get ice cream at Baskin Robbins and when you are faced with the choice of 31 flavors, you feel overwhelmed.

I apologize. We were talking about cycling and bikes, but really we are talking about choices. The choices we make every day affect our lives for good or for bad. A series of bad choices can lead to destruction. In that same way, a series of really good choices can lead us down a road of success and happiness. So how do we know whether or not we are making the right choices in our lives?

Consider the outcome of the choices you make. If I go out for a leisurely ride, I am not looking for roads with challenging hills; I want smooth, level roads. On the other hand, if I am going out for a training ride, I may want to work on hills. But either way, I am planning ahead for what will fit and what I desire to accomplish. Both are paths I can choose, but depending on my mindset I may be disappointed in the end.

Not every choice is easy, but one choice is clear in the Bible and that is life. God's word tells us He sets life and death before us and then He tells us which one to choose: life! It is the obvious answer, but for whatever reason we sometimes make the wrong choice and experience some form of death in our lives. But when we choose life, we experience life and live more abundantly. That is the promise of Jesus. He did not say that every day would be easy, but He gives us abundant life when we choose to follow Him.

So the next time you are planning out your ride and going through all the choices you have to make on your route, think about this: What choice can you make to improve your riding experience today? If it is simply modifying your route a little, then do it. When you get back from your ride and you feel better about the choices you made, think about this: Where can you apply this same principle of choice in your life to make things better?

Remember the five essentials and take one thing that you know you could do. Maybe it's a relationship and you just need to make that call. Maybe it's a visit to your doctor or your dentist. Just make the call. The power of choice is one that God has given each one of us, and it truly is a powerful force when we make the right choices. I believe that anyone can do this and it will help your attitude, your health, your finances and your relationships. That is the power behind the cycle of choice. Consistently well thought out choices can change you forever! Choose life and you will live, really live!

(*Deuteronomy 30:15-20*)

Review and Reflect
- Life is a choice.
- We all have a lot of choices.
- A series of choices can make us or break us.
- Consistently well thought out choices can change us forever.
- There is really only one choice.
- Choose life.

Quotable Quote

"The power of choice is the power of change!"
"I don't just slay my giants, I ride one!"

Cycling Log

Bike/Type _____ Day _____ Month _____ Year _____

Weather: ☐ Sunny ☐ Cloudy ☐ Windy ☐ Rain ☐ Snow ☐ Other

Read: Topic of the day

_____

_____

Ride and Record

Miles _____ Route _____

Time _____ Average Speed _____

Revolt

Change, goals, thoughts of the day

_____

_____

_____

_____

_____

- 31-day reading plan: Proverbs 12

Day 12 - The Road Less Traveled

I recently wrote down this statement: "Start where you are, go to where you haven't been, come back to where you need to be." So often we get stuck in a routine that is not always bad but may not afford us the best perspective. Every once in a while it's good to take the road less traveled. If your routine is to always start your ride from the same place, and you take the same route every day, you might get bored. I try to find new routes to give me a change of scenery. I still have to get back to where the car is parked, but I will have seen a different part of town, passed people I had never seen before, or ridden up a challenging hill.

The reality is that often our routine can get mundane and we need to free up our minds by breaking up the cycle and getting a change of scenery. This might mean changing your weekly rest cycle or simply venturing out of your comfort zone and finding other possibilities. The great news is that when we do this, it gives us a new perspective on life. It doesn't have to be hard, but it is necessary.

Breaking bad habits means venturing out beyond where you are so that you can get to where you need to be. This is how you revolt. The amazing thing is that it can be as easy as taking a rest day when you wouldn't normally. Any time you are working towards change, it is your mindset or your thought processes that need to be challenged. Ask yourself hard questions like, "Why am I doing this?" Be honest with yourself and write down what you think. Then ask, "What can I do to change?" Just by doing this you are actively working toward change.

I am reminded of God's word. "As the heavens are higher than the earth, so are my ways higher than your ways and my thoughts than your thoughts." (*Isaiah 55:9*) To think like God is to think outside the box and test our comfort zone. Riding is the same. When we take an unfamiliar route, we tend to be more alert about what is around us and pay close attention to the path. Isn't that the basis of what we should have been doing all along, paying attention?
Psalms 23

Review and Reflect
- Start where you are. Every small step matters.
- Explore a new route. This allows you to see new things outside your comfort zone.
- Come back to where you need to be. You know what needs to change. Just do it!
- Pay attention. You can learn a lot when you focus.

Quotable Quote

"The road less traveled has no beaten path so prepare to pedal."

Cycling Log

Bike/Type _____ Day _____ Month _____ Year _____

Weather: ☐ Sunny ☐ Cloudy ☐ Windy ☐ Rain ☐ Snow ☐ Other

Read: Topic of the day

_____

_____

Ride and Record

Miles _____ Route _____

Time _____ Average Speed _____

Revolt

Change, goals, thoughts of the day

_____

_____

_____

_____

_____

_____

• 31-day reading plan: Proverbs 13

Day 13 - Face Plant -
A Downhill Story

It's still there, the scar that shows the daredevil I used to be. My forehead still bears the mark and memory of a young boy showing off with a neighborhood friend. What was so cool about taking both hands off the handlebars while cruising down a hill? Well it was freeing! To let go of the controls and succumb to the thrill of balance and speed on a hill I had gone down dozens of times. But this day was different. I forgot about the bump that would cause my front tire to jump back and forth in uncontrollable frenzy.

And there I was with nowhere to go but down, reaching desperately for the handlebars. I made a perfect face plant onto the hard surface of an Oklahoma blacktop road. It happened so fast my buddy just missed my head by inches as he zoomed by. The once new BMX bike I was riding began bouncing recklessly down the hill until it stopped several yards from where I was. I loved that bike. It was so cool!

I quickly jumped to my feet as if nothing was wrong. My buddy was in shock and ripped off his shirt to wipe all the blood coming from my face. A car was passing by, and when I turned my head to get a better look, it stopped immediately. "Get in! We will take you home," the driver said. Reluctantly, I got in the back seat.

My buddy said, "I'll get the bike. Don't worry about it."

When I got home, my mom was waiting for me. The sight that greeted me in the full length mirror of the family bathroom was not a pretty one. "You are going to need stitches," mom explained.

"No, I don't want to get stitches," I said, as if I had any say in things. After arguing with her about how I didn't want to go, she loaded me in the car and off we went. It wasn't my first time and unfortunately not my last. It seems it takes me more than one face plant to learn. The next one, however, would be on a trampoline!

But the last one was the worst, and though I bear no physical scars, the real scars are hidden within. It was my own pride and haughtiness that caused this fall, and it took me a great deal of time to overcome and understand this. The Bible clearly warns us about such things, but because we are human, we somehow think we are immune to the bumps life dishes out. Nothing could be further from the truth.

This is why it is so important for us to regularly check in on our core values. What is going on inside can really mess us up. My downhill face plant comes to mind! I have fully recovered from all of my injuries, including the self inflicted wounds to my own pride. But some of the physical scars remain to remind me of the road I have traveled. They are there to remind me and to warn others of the dangers of letting go of things we can and should control. And then there is the flip side of letting go of the things we need to entrust to God.

If you incline your heart to wisdom, you can avoid the pitfalls of foolishness and save face! Literally! "Whoever has ears, let them hear." (*Matthew 11:15*)

Sometimes we can't see our own reflection, even when it is right in front of us. The sad thing is that what we see should alarm us before we go any further. Blindness happens gradually, when we don't stop to do some thoughtful self-examination. What you can't see, others will, so don't be surprised when they point something out because they are watching. Don't be offended. If you are, let that be a red flag. I highly recommend watching for flags! Otherwise, I can tell you that the pavement will break your fall!

Psalms 51:10-12

Review and Reflect

- Pride goes before a fall (or face plant).
- Self-examination can save face.
- Check your vision. Your reflection could be telling you something.
- If you can't see it, others will point it out to you.
- Don't be offended. Watch for red flags and bumps in the road!

Quotable Quote

The white flag of surrender should be used if we begin to see red flags in our lives! Check yourself before you wreck yourself!

Cycling Log

Bike/Type _____ Day _____ Month _____ Year _____
Weather: ☐ Sunny ☐ Cloudy ☐ Windy ☐ Rain ☐ Snow ☐ Other
Read: Topic of the day

_____

_____

Ride and Record

Miles _____ Route _____

Time _____ Average Speed _____

Revolt
Change, goals, thoughts of the day

_____

_____

_____

_____

_____

_____

- 31-day reading plan: Proverbs 14

Day 14 - The Trinity Cycle

When I think about the word trinity, three things come to mind: the trinity of God, the trinity of man and the trinity cycle. The trinity of God is represented by God the Father, God the son and God the Holy Spirit. (*1 John 5:7*) The trinity of man is made up of spirit, soul and body. (*Mark 12:30*) The trinity cycle is made up of three critical cycles: the revolutions cycle, the rewards cycle and the rest cycle. In this discussion, we will discuss this last trinity.

I have been talking a lot about the revolution cycle, and I want to define it as the work cycle. This is where the rubber literally hits the road. For this cycle to work for you, you have to work. There are no excuses to be made for it—this is just the way it is. But at the end of the work cycle there is a great reward, which takes us to the next cycle, the reward cycle.

We have not discussed this cycle at all because it is a new concept but an important one. The rewards cycle is what we live on after our revolution. It is the lute of our battle. At some point, change becomes a habit, and it no longer has an effect on your outcome or goal. That is when you put it into the reward cycle and live off the fruits of your reward.

So how do you get into the rest cycle? You probably just passed by it and didn't even realize it was there. It is the place of rest beyond the work and the reward. Why can you rest? Because you have done the work, reaped the rewards and entered into the rest. You have made the change, and it doesn't have the power to affect you again. Isn't that awesome? Trying to capture this concept kept me up one Christmas Eve and well into Christmas Day. The truth in this is so real in so many areas of our lives. At some point, you get over things that once held you down, but now you rest, as I will once I am finished writing this.

Here is my prayer for you as you are reading this right now. I pray the trinity cycle will have an effect on your life spiritually, physically and mentally, that it will create change in your spirit, soul and body and bring you into the rest God has for you!

John 4:24, Deuteronomy 6:4-7, Luke 10:27

Review and Reflect
- Trinity of God: Father, Son, Holy Spirit.
- Trinity of man: spirit, soul, body.
- Trinity cycle: revolutions, reward, rest.
- Good habits reap good habits.

Quotable Quote

"The risk of a revolution is worth the reward and rest at the end of it."

Cycling Log

Bike/Type _____ Day _____ Month _____ Year _____

Weather: ☐ Sunny ☐ Cloudy ☐ Windy ☐ Rain ☐ Snow ☐ Other

Read: Topic of the day

_____

_____

Ride and Record

Miles _____ Route _____

Time _____ Average Speed _____

Revolt

Change, goals, thoughts of the day

_____

_____

_____

_____

_____

_____

• 31-day reading plan: Proverbs 15

Inspiration

What inspires you today? This is a great question to ask right now. It often takes inspiration to motivate us to action. Cycling inspired me to write this book because of the changes I was seeing in my own life. I wondered if cycling could make a difference in my mental and physical condition and what other areas could it affect? And how could I use this platform to inspire others? That's all it took to get me inspired!

Maybe your story is similar, or maybe you are inspired by something totally different, but cycling has put us on common ground. That's what I like about the bike. It puts people in a common place, and a community is built around it. We don't have to have the same goals, the same beliefs, the same values or the same kind of bike. We just have to love it! That puts us in a place to work together and overcome the obstacles we are facing.

What obstacles are you facing right now? Write them down so you can begin to work on the solutions to those obstacles. You can do it if you believe you can. That core value of believing in yourself is so important. The more you love yourself, the more you can learn to love others more completely. You have also got to love that bike or find one that you do love!

Without inspiration, life can become pretty dull. I love true stories of inspiration, even though they may bring me to tears. That is the power of inspiration. It touches the deep part of our soul that needs to be moved. The tears are part of relating to the story of our own struggle with life cycles. So it's okay to shed a tear or two and begin to open up our own hearts and minds to the possibilities of victory!

I hope you get inspired today to win! To overcome every obstacle you are facing, whether it is a sickness or disease or a life-changing decision. Be inspired! Be empowered to overcome by your own decision right now. The future is dependent upon your choice at this very moment. You will need it to gain momentum for what is ahead of you. In the Bible, David picked five stones up from the river bed, but it only took one from his sling to slay his giant. David didn't pick up five stones because he thought he would miss on his first few attempts, he was looking into his future beyond Goliath, because he knew he had brothers!

That is how we need to face our future—knowing that the current struggle is only temporary. Prepare to know that it won't be the last. It's always good to get past that first obstacle because it makes the next few easier to face. We add confidence to our courage every time we face our giants and win!

Quotable Quote

"Your inspiration is in your next battle, slay the doubt!"

Cycling Log

Bike/Type _____ Day _____ Month _____ Year _____
Weather: ☐ Sunny ☐ Cloudy ☐ Windy ☐ Rain ☐ Snow ☐ Other
Read: Topic of the day

_____

_____

Ride and Record

Miles _____ Route _____

Time _____ Average Speed _____

Revolt
Change, goals, thoughts of the day

_____

_____

_____

_____

_____

_____

- 31-day reading plan: Proverbs 16

Week 3 – Performance Principles

Day 15 - More to the Core

D eep down, it is important for you to know who you are and what you believe. Knowing your true nature will help establish where you are going in life. Your core beliefs are also defined by your worldview because this becomes the filter through which you process the thoughts that determine your actions.

My decisions are the engine that propels change. The statements "I want to change" or "I need to change" are both statements with no action. But when I make a conscious decision to change, write it down and start working toward a goal, then something begins to turn. My attitude is different, as is my outlook. I don't want to stay where I am, so I take steps toward my goal to get me to another location that looks and feels like where I desire to be. Real lasting change is a process of decisions that has to be repeated over and over again until it becomes a habit that is hard to break. That's when you discover breakthrough!

Your core or axis is centered around and controlled by your beliefs. Everything that revolves around you will be affected by this belief system. It is important that this system is healthy or it will cause problems in every area of your life, including cycling. I would suggest checking in on a monthly basis to see how you are doing at your core. Ask yourself and others to get real feedback to determine your core fitness.

Discovering areas of weakness is not a bad thing. Even the apostle Paul spoke of his weakness, but his belief system made him strong. "For when I am weak, then I am strong." (*2 Corinthians 12:9-11*) At some point we have to realize the shortcomings we have to overcome. If we think everything is great all the time, we may miss the very change that will elevate us to the next level. Examination is a skill based in faith, one that we need to work on that will keep us healthy and humble deep inside. Paul wrote: "Do your best to present yourself to God as one approved." (*2 Timothy 2:15*) Jesus said we should examine our own heart and motives before examining others. (*Matthew 7:1*). Pride is weakness and humility is strength! Two passages in the Bible help us with this one: *Proverbs 16:18, James 4:10.*

One thing I remind myself and keep at my core is this realization that it's not about me. In Rick Warren's book, "The Purpose Driven Life" this is one of his first points. If we learn and understand that our purpose is bigger than ourselves, we will live a much happier and fulfilled life. On your ride today, think about your purpose in life. Is there more to the core of who I say and believe I am? Find the answer and write it down, and if you already know your purpose, then stay humble, because you are on the road to success and on the ride of your life!

Review and Reflect

- Your core is your axis. It defines who you are, what you believe and the decisions you make.
- Your decisions are determined by your belief system.
- Examination is a skill and needed for a healthy core.
- Weaknesses are an opportunity for growth.
- Humility is a must for change.

Quotable Quote

"Humility is the strength that pride attempts to obtain on its own!"

Cycling Log

Bike/Type _____ Day _____ Month _____ Year _____

Weather: ☐ Sunny ☐ Cloudy ☐ Windy ☐ Rain ☐ Snow ☐ Other

Read: Topic of the day

_____

_____

Ride and Record

Miles _____ Route _____

Time _____ Average Speed _____

Revolt

Change, goals, thoughts of the day

_____

_____

_____

_____

_____

_____

• 31-day reading plan: Proverbs 17

Day 16 - Broken Spokes

It was a red Schwinn twelve-speed, most likely a model from the late 80's to early 90's. I had bought it on Craigslist, a classified advertisements website, and it was my first road bike, the one I wanted to use to start training and just enjoy riding. The mountain bike I had been riding just wasn't cutting it for the road any more. There was a duathlon[2] coming up in the fall that I wanted to participate in, so this was going to be my experience.

How quickly time flies! Before I knew it, I'd rolled into my second season, and I was riding regularly. This day was no different from any other hot summer in Oklahoma. There was a clicking noise that had begun to annoy me the last few times I had ridden my bike. Because I was still new to riding, I didn't give it much thought, so I never took the time to discover the source of the problem. Today I would find out the source of any unusual sound coming from my bike.

---

[2]   A duathlon is a sporting event that consists of a running leg followed by a cycling leg and then another running leg.

I was on my lunch break and was headed back to the mill after riding several miles when I heard the pop. With only half a mile to go, my bike started wobbling all over the road. I looked at my back wheel in disbelief. I saw not one, or even two, but three broken spokes! This had never happened to me before! I'd had flat tires, but never broken spokes. The funny thing is that after walking the bike back, my buddy told me he'd had a similar experience. So if you ride enough, broken spokes are as much of a possibility as flat tires.

What else in our lives can break over time if we are not paying attention? Relationships come to mind. If we don't maintain them, they can begin to show signs of wear and tear. It's important to stop and examine the spokes and folks in our lives. Broken spokes and folks have a lot in common. Your world won't turn as smoothly when the connections between your hub and rim are broken.

At your hub are your core values, and they are the connection to the folks within your sphere of influence. If the spokes of your communication are broken, your world will begin to wobble and spin out of control. Your relationships provide your wheels with the strength you need to get you to where you need to be. Until it is broken, one spoke may seem insignificant. The same holds true with the people in our lives. Trust me when I say that you will need every spoke and every folk in your life as you move forward towards your goal.

Relationships help us define a reason for our purpose. Whether the relationships are with our family, friends or coworkers, they play an important role in our development as a person. Mentors along the way, such as pastors, teachers and employers, all have a hand in our success. Parents had a huge role in my life as they helped build the foundation of faith and work ethic in my life. Folks are for living and spokes are for riding. We need them both to maintain balance on the road of life.

Psalms 51:17

Review and Reflect
* You are connected to folks.
* Your core is connected to your circle of influence.
* Relationships need maintenance.
* Relationships help us define the why to our purpose.

Quotable Quote

"Folks are the spokes in our circle of influence we need."

Cycling Log

Bike/Type _____ Day _____ Month _____ Year _____

Weather: ☐ Sunny ☐ Cloudy ☐ Windy ☐ Rain ☐ Snow ☐ Other

Read: Topic of the day

_____

_____

Ride and Record

Miles _____ Route _____

Time _____ Average Speed _____

Revolt

Change, goals, thoughts of the day

_____

_____

_____

_____

_____

_____

• 31-day reading plan: Proverbs 18

Day 17 - A Glimpse into the Past

L ast Christmas I got a glimpse into my past that I didn't really remember. My sister had made a DVD of old home movies for the whole family. I discovered the footage of myself riding an old bike around in the front yard of our old farm house. What surprised me is that I was barefoot and about five or six years old. I actually recognized the bike I was riding from an earlier clip. It was a bike my older brother had gotten for his birthday a few years earlier. It's amazing what you rediscover when you look back on your life!

The bike I vaguely remembered is the same bike I first learned to ride on. Later on I got my own bike, and yet I can barely recall what it looked like or when I got it. I do remember the long, red, sparkly vinyl seat and big handle bars with red grips. I must have gotten it for my fifth or sixth birthday because my first ride to town was when I was in kindergarten. I was riding with my brother, Tom, who was in the fifth grade at that time.

We lived just two and a half miles from town on a fair-sized hill. You don't really notice the size of the hill on your way into town. That day and that ride was a disaster for me. I crashed at least twice going down the freshly graveled hill. This was about five years before my face plant on that same hill after it had been asphalted. Great memories embedded in my mind and in my skin!

You might ask where this story is headed. As I looked back on that film of me going around in circles under the big maple tree, I realized how long I have had the ability to ride. How often life brings us full circle or a full revolution and lets us see something new in something old.

Today I don't ride barefoot. The bikes have changed, but the smile I had is still there when I get on my bike to ride. There is a youthfulness tied to riding that I can't really explain. But taking me back leads me forward, and I know I want to enjoy the days ahead as well as celebrate the moment I am currently in.

It's worth looking inside yourself and determining if you are truly happy with the now. Do you feel fulfillment in the dreams and passions that cause you to live each day? Can you smile, even when you realize you just made a huge circle in the front yard of your life and are right back where you began?

I wonder what I was thinking as I performed for the camera on that day. I am just thankful it got captured so I could see where I came from and reach a better understanding about where I am headed. The Bible really helps me to understand God's purpose for my life.

Jeremiah 29:11

Review and Reflect

* A glimpse into the past can tell us a story.
* We often find ourselves in the circle of life.
* What really causes you to live?
* What are your dreams and passions?

Quotable Quote

"Going around in circles is fine if you know the why to why you are doing it."

Cycling Log

Bike/Type _____ Day _____ Month _____ Year _____

Weather: ☐ Sunny ☐ Cloudy ☐ Windy ☐ Rain ☐ Snow ☐ Other

Read: Topic of the day

_____

_____

Ride and Record

Miles _____ Route _____

Time _____ Average Speed _____

Revolt

Change, goals, thoughts of the day

_____

_____

_____

_____

_____

_____

- 31-day reading plan: Proverbs 19

Day 18 - A B C Cycle

T he alphabet is a great place to start because singing your ABCs is as easy as 1-2-3. I first learned these principles from the Bible. This is what ABC represents for me:

- Admit there is a problem
- Believe there is a solution
- Commit to change

This is how it works in relationship to becoming a believer in the Christian faith:

- Admit you are a sinner. (*Romans 3:23*)
- Believe in the Lord Jesus Christ as your savior. (*Romans 6:23*)
- Declare with your mouth "Jesus Christ is Lord," and believe in your heart for your salvation. (*Romans 10:9,10 and 10:13*)

Profound truth is found in these steps, steps that sound so unbelievably easy. The longer I live, the more I understand how little I know, and yet I still find simple is better. It is not so much that the first steps are terribly hard, it is the thousands more we will take. This applies to cycling as well. There are many more revolutions to go.

Many people are looking for the X Y Z without first doing the A B Cs. In the process you leave out the D T W. What does all this mean? Living life to the fullest, really thriving in everything we do is the X Y Z, or X-treme Years of Zest! The gap in between is the one no one wants to face, but it is "the what" that brings it all together. D T W stands for "Do the Work." If you don't do the first steps, you can never enjoy the rewards of the end result.

Today you may be at the beginning of the alphabet and you need to realize some things. Admitting you have a problem that you can't solve on your own opens the door of opportunity for help. Believing there is a solution is the best thing. You will find out that you are not alone and that others can show you how they solved the same problem. Then make the commitment to yourself. This is about your own revolution and the possibilities that come your way because of change. One decision can change your life forever!

The truth is that God valued your life enough to give you His only son to take your place for the penalty you deserved. Remember today as you ride to put value on your life and invest in yourself every day. And then begin to value those around you and invest in them. When we start to do this, our life starts a transformation that leads to revolutions!

Romans 3:23, 3:10-18, 6:23, 5:8, 10:9, 10:13, 5:1, 8:1, 8:38-39

Review and Reflect
- Admit there is a problem.
- Believe in a solution.
- Commit to change.
- DTW. Do the work.
- Place value on your life.

Quotable Quote

"What you value is what you will invest in."

Cycling Log

Bike/Type _____ Day _____ Month _____ Year _____

Weather: ☐ Sunny ☐ Cloudy ☐ Windy ☐ Rain ☐ Snow ☐ Other

Read: Topic of the day

_____

_____

Ride and Record

Miles _____ Route _____

Time _____ Average Speed _____

Revolt

Change, goals, thoughts of the day

_____

_____

_____

_____

_____

_____

• 31-day reading plan: Proverbs 20

Day 19 - The Upside to Hills

W e've all experienced it. The anxiety we face at the upcoming hills and then the burning sensation in all our muscles! A couple of years ago, I remember passing the caution sign that read "Hills Ahead." I had to laugh because I knew that just like in life it could prove to be difficult at first, but somehow I would push through the burning. I also knew that a reward would await me on the other side. I returned to the sign to take a picture that would serve as a reminder that the challenge will still be there the next time.

Today I have learned to navigate the small hills and also learned to enjoy them. Not only have they helped build my strength, they have given me pleasure. When I approach a hill, I have to remind myself of the joy on the other side. While climbing may be painful, it can reap some great benefits in the end.

The view is always better from the top of the mountain. And if you are willing to ascend, the descent can be invigorating! Woody Guthrie wrote the song "Oklahoma Hills," and for the most part, hills are a fundamental part of the Oklahoma experience. In contrast, Colorado, which borders the Oklahoma Panhandle, is mountainous.

It's hard for us to imagine the "Rocky Mountain High" that John Denver sang about.

Last year, my friend made the trip to Pikes Peak[3] so he could descend the giant on his road bike. That thought had never crossed my mind, but I thought it was pretty cool. It was only the start of his second riding season, so this was a big deal. Before his ride, he did some altitude training, knowing there would be a lack of oxygen up there.

I was working when the text came to me with his picture next to the sign at the crest of Pikes Peak. He was wearing the golden jersey he had won for bragging rights the month before. After outriding us in May by more than 100 miles, I decided he had earned it! The next text was a picture of him cruising down the road on his road bike, a Specialized, with the beautiful Rockies in the background.

Here's one thing about mountaintop experiences: you never will get enough! A few months later he made another trip, this time to South Dakota to ride with the backdrop of Mount Rushmore[4]. It's amazing what a difference a bike can make on a vacation. Again, making a trip like this had never really crossed my mind but way to go Danny!

Not everybody wants to take the high road or scale the highest mountain. But we all want those mountaintop moments so we can experience the vantage point from above, overlooking the valleys below. Isn't this true in our own lives? What can we learn from hills? There is always an upside to climbing hills. In contrast to the struggle of climbing the hill, we enjoy the descent that much more.

---

[3] Pikes Peak is the highest summit of the southern Front Range of the Rocky Mountains.

[4] Mount Rushmore National Memorial is a massive sculpture carved into Mt. Rushmore in the Black Hills region of South Dakota.

Sooner or later we have to learn to embrace the climb, without which we won't be able to enjoy the view and the descent.

You're no doubt familiar with the saying, "Don't make mountains out of mole hills." This is like comparing the hills around Tulsa, Oklahoma to the mountain ranges of Colorado. There is no comparison. But if we use every hill we climb as training ground to prepare us for the mountains, we will learn to overcome our struggles.

Large goals need to be broken down into smaller, achievable ones. After a series of small climbs, we can see we have achieved a chunk of our larger goal. Every challenge we face in life needs to be dealt with the same way, one at a time, climb by climb. Eventually we will find ourselves at the top of every situation.

Mark 11:23-24

Review and Reflect
* There are always hills ahead.
* Learn to navigate the small hills.
* Mountain top experiences will come.
* Endure the ascent so you can enjoy the descent.
* The view is better from the top.

Quotable Quote

*"Remember mountain visions include
hillside scenery along the way."*

Cycling Log

Bike/Type _____ Day _____ Month _____ Year _____

Weather: ☐ Sunny ☐ Cloudy ☐ Windy ☐ Rain ☐ Snow ☐ Other

Read: Topic of the day

_____

_____

Ride and Record

Miles _____ Route _____

Time _____ Average Speed _____

Revolt

Change, goals, thoughts of the day

_____

_____

_____

_____

_____

_____

- 31-day reading plan: Proverbs 21

Day 20 - Chain Reaction

The phrase "it started a chain reaction" usually has a negative connotation for me. I would like to take you down that road for a moment. It's important to get a visual on this subject.

Last year I was religiously riding my bike every day. From April 30 to November 26, I didn't miss a single day of riding. Not all the rides were long ones, but I did log about 3,400 miles during that time and finished the year with just over 4,400 miles.

During that time, I began to have some issues with shifting. More importantly, I was having some maintenance issues. Ignoring the signs of wear and tear, I just kept on pedaling away. Maintaining my bike hasn't always been my top priority.

Finally, in the last week of September, I took my bike in for a tune up, since the annual duathlon was the first weekend of October. I told the bicycle mechanic I wanted to put on a new chain. When he slipped his gauge over my chain, he commented that the chain was so worn out it didn't even measure. He also commented that it was so dry he wondered if I ever oiled it.

I left the bike overnight. I was told to be prepared that the new chain might slip. I returned on a Thursday to pick up the bike. My event was on Sunday. He said to take it out for a test ride to check the shifting. The bike looked great. It had a clean, new chain. I was ready to go.

100 yards into my ride, I felt a slip, and then another one. I kept shifting around trying to find a spot that would work. Sure enough, the lower gears seemed to be shifting fine, but the gears I used the most were slipping.

I returned to the bike shop after a couple of disappointing miles and explained what was going on. The owner asked me if it was in the mid-range gears, and I replied in the affirmative. He knew exactly what was going on. The worn out chain had ruined my cassette and it would need to be replaced.

Fortunately for me, they had one and replaced it right away, so that I would have a chance to ride and adjust anything if necessary. It did need some slight adjustments, and I was able to do these on my own. Once these were done, the chain and cassette worked seamlessly.

The moral of the story is that maintenance is required in life and in biking. A to-do list and discipline are all a part of a successful maintenance program and mindset. If you keep a list and follow that list, you won't get worn, dry and stretched out trying to retain things that you could have written down.

Just the other day, I found something I'd written several years ago that still resonates with me. The word SAD stands for Schedule, Appointments and Deadlines. We are all bound by them. If we don't meet our obligations, we might find ourselves needing more than just a routine tune up!

The positive side of a chain reaction is that when things are scheduled and maintained regularly, they come together like a chain and sprocket. That is what will help propel us towards the place we want to reach in all areas of our life. A series of good decisions starts a chain reaction that can change our current situation.

Romans 13:8 Psalms 89:28

Review and Reflect
* Maintenance is a must.
* Check your chain.
* A to do list is a must.
* Have the discipline to follow through.
* SAD: Schedules, Appointments, Deadlines

Quotable Quote

"Maintain the chain. It is the link to pull you through life!"

Cycling Log

Bike/Type _____ Day _____ Month _____ Year _____

Weather: ☐ Sunny ☐ Cloudy ☐ Windy ☐ Rain ☐ Snow ☐ Other

Read: Topic of the day

_____

_____

Ride and Record

Miles _____ Route _____

Time _____ Average Speed _____

Revolt

Change, goals, thoughts of the day

_____

_____

_____

_____

_____

- 31-day reading plan: Proverbs 22

96

Day 21 - Back to the Basics

We've all heard the saying, "It's as easy as riding a bike - once you've done it you never forget how." So what is the greatest and basic principle for riding a bike? In my opinion it has to be balance, and the same is true in life. Finding balance in our everyday schedule throughout life can be a difficult challenge.

Juggling and riding a bike is optimal for a circus act but not for a parent trying to set an example for their kids. Although it may feel like a three-ring circus at times, we need to get back to the basics and establish some balance before we crash!

The best place to start is with a plan, a map to help you better navigate through your day. Day planners are set up just for that. They get you organized and let you put together a to-do list. I always start with the most important things that need to be done now, and then I throw in every little thing I can think of that needs to get done. If my list doesn't all get done today at least I have something to start with tomorrow and something that shows what I finished today.

Your task is to manage your day better and not let it manage you. Trying to keep all the things you need to do in your head is hard and not practical, no matter what you age. The better you become at writing things down, the more you can see your accomplishments. If you write nothing down at the end of the day, how do you know if you accomplished what you needed too? That's why this book will become a great asset to you. It will train you to write things down and record activities.

As we follow the trend of planning out our day, carry that into the month and stretch it out over a year. Looking forward is a good way to maintain balance. Staying focused on what is in front of you, not looking to your left or your right, not being distracted as you go. When distractions come, as they will, return to the original plan you wrote down that day. Follow-through is important to your success.

So how do we achieve the balance we need to ride through this journey called life? First, we need a plan to direct us in our path, to guide us to where we are going. Second, we need to write things down so we aren't wasting energy trying to remember everything we need to do. This way we can measure our success as we achieve our goals. The third and final point is to stay focused on the task at hand. You will not finish what you do not stay focused on. You can have a plan in your head, but until you write it down it is only an idea, one that cannot be realized or materialized. If it is not written it is not relevant.

Habakkuk 2:2, 1 Samuel 18:14

Review and Reflect
- Make a plan: Get a day planner.
- Write it down. This will be your to-do-list.
- Stay focused on the task at hand.
- Follow through for success.

Quotable Quote

"If it is not written it is not relevant, realized or materialized."

Cycling Log

Bike/Type _____ Day _____ Month _____ Year _____

Weather: ☐ Sunny ☐ Cloudy ☐ Windy ☐ Rain ☐ Snow ☐ Other

Read: Topic of the day

_____

_____

Ride and Record

Miles _____ Route _____

Time _____ Average Speed _____

Revolt

Change, goals, thoughts of the day

_____

_____

_____

_____

_____

_____

• 31-day reading plan: Proverbs 23

Week 4 – A Successful Mindset

Day 22 - Connections

This may be one of the most important keys to your success. Connection is about people, not just any people, but the people who are most important to you. The people you are connected to will determine your success. I touched a little on this subject in *Broken Spokes*, but I'd like to explore the importance of connections a bit more deeply here. When I refer to those in our circle, I am not just talking about the ones we influence but also the ones who influence us. This goes beyond our immediate family and into the great unknown of social media as well as other ways we can connect.

When it comes to determining our path of success, the people we meet along the way and the people we connect with are important. How we listen to these individuals and interact with them will either carry us a long way or stop us short of our goals. Pay attention to those you encounter and ask yourself a few questions. Why is this person in my life at this time? What is my relationship with this person going to be? Who is this person connected to that we both may need? How is this connection important to my success? When do I know this connection is important enough to maintain?

Now let's be real for a moment. These are tough questions, and we don't always have the answers to them. It makes me wish there was an app like MapQuest (a free online web mapping service) where I could just punch in the info and realize where this is all going! That is part of the journey we have to take when we make connections. Some connections become the links in our chain, some the spokes in our wheels and others the nails in our tires! So that is why it is necessary to figure out the value of those you are connected to. Not every relationship is perfect, and some relationships are there to help perfect us.

It's easy to build a large friendship base on social media, but it is much harder to find true friends. How many of your Facebook friends would show up to carry your casket? That may seem a little harsh, but how many will drop everything and come help you move on the only free weekend they've had in several months. Thankfully, I have encountered friends like that in my life. And how many friends will really pray for you when you ask? I have those as well.

Family, friends and fellow citizens are all part of the world we are connected with. They make our world go around many times and help us see our own faults so that we can better ourselves. That's what good people do. They make life better for themselves and the ones they love. Sometimes the difference between a better you and finding success is the person right in front of you. Connect on some level and explore where you can go.

Finally, I want to mention my greatest connection on earth. I will be celebrating 30 years this year with my wife Brenda. The only way I can describe our connection is that it had to be God! Little did I know that some 30 years ago I would become connected to the most beautiful woman I know. She is beautiful both within and without. She has been my friend and my lover through countless good times and a few bad times as well. Without a doubt, she still moves my heart and puts a twinkle in my eye. She is the mother of our beautiful and intelligent daughter Gabrielle. Together we are a small but loving family, the most important connection for me and my life here on earth.

With my relationship with my wife and daughter, my faith in God, and my connection to the road on my bike, life doesn't get much better for me, unless you count all the other people. It is clear to me that every year God places more and more people in my life who are making an impact on me. I am so thankful for that and continue to welcome those connections as I look for meaningful relationships that will help me grow as a person. In life we often tend to pedal past the people God intended us to pedal with. My advice: pay close attention and get connected!

Luke 5:17-26

Review and Reflect

- Connections are important.
- Your success depends on people.
- Ask the questions.
- Seek meaningful relationships.
- Pay close attention and get connected.

Quotable Quote

"True friends will carry your couch or your casket, whichever move comes first!"

Cycling Log

Bike/Type _____ Day _____ Month _____ Year _____

Weather: ☐ Sunny ☐ Cloudy ☐ Windy ☐ Rain ☐ Snow ☐ Other

Read: Topic of the day

_____

_____

Ride and Record

Miles _____ Route _____

Time _____ Average Speed _____

Revolt

Change, goals, thoughts of the day

_____

_____

_____

_____

_____

_____

• 31-day reading plan: Proverbs 24

Day 23 - A Success Story

I recently had the opportunity to interview my brother-in-law, a life-long educator, teacher, coach and administrator. The intent was to glean from him the story of his success. For me it was a great conversation that gave me a clearer insight to his life.

As a kid, Monte grew up moving a lot due to an unstable home life. You would have thought this to be uncommon in the 50s and 60s, but he experienced it firsthand. Fortunately, he enjoyed a few years of stability in high school, and this is where he first got a glimpse of what he wanted to do. It was the high school teachers and coaches of the small town of Berryhill, Oklahoma who caught his attention.

After high school, Monte served his country in the Air National Guard[5] while working his way through college. It was in college where he learned one of the important habits of a successful person. He carried lists in his shirt pocket and always had a pen ready to write down the next thing to do. I asked him about that, and he told

---

5   The Air National Guard is a federal military reserve force as well as the militia air force of each U.S. state.

me it was a habit that started early. He had to write things down, or he would forget. This helped him keep up with his daily school schedule.

He got his first teaching job in 1971, and he found himself back at home in Berryhill. Shortly thereafter, he made his way to Haskell, where his coaching career in girls' high school began. This wasn't his first choice because he had always loved football, but it became the obvious path to his success. Winning become a tradition, and he earned a 113-26 record over a five-year period. This opened the door to his next big step. In 1979, he took on the challenge of becoming a junior college coach at Connors State College in Warner, Oklahoma. This would prove to be the way Monte Madewell would leave his mark on women's basketball in Oklahoma for the next 20 years!

He had an illustrious coaching career. During his time at Connors State College, he coached his team to a record of 547 wins and only 121 losses, resulting in an 82 percent winning average. That accounted for an average of 27 games per season. He had a 73 home game winning streak that spanned about eight years. He earned a national championship title in 1985 and runner-up in 1989, with a 103-2 home record. He was also named National Junior College Athletic Association (NJCAA) Coach of the Year in 1985 and coached the NJCAA All-Star game that same year. The list goes on: 17 NJCAA All-Americans, two NJCAA players of the year and many Academic All-Americans[6]. They were ranked number one in seven different seasons and recorded many other wins along the way, both in conference and tournament appearances. During all this time, he was also the Athletic Director at Connors State College.

In 2002, Monte was inducted into the Oklahoma High School Coaches Hall of Fame, and in 2009 he was inducted into the NJCAA

---

[6] An Academic All-American is an award granted to an American college student who has met certain criteria in terms of academic and athletic accomplishments.

Coaches Hall of Fame. In 2014, he was also inducted into Connors State College Hall of Fame. After holding only two head coaching jobs, his overall record was 660-147. After retiring from coaching in 2001, he continued to contribute to education for another 11 years as a superintendent in his hometown of Warner.

You might be wondering what all this has to do with cycling. I believe that as we go through the cycles of life, opportunities present themselves, and we have to decide what we will do with them. In his case, Monte always followed his heart, and it led him well. Each decision involved weighing out the pros and the cons. Success can be part of our cycling experience if we pay attention at every turn.

I asked Monte how he would sum up his success, and he said it all came down to the relationships he built along the way. It was the meaningful relationships that made the success what it really was meant to be. This probably never made the list in his pocket, but it became the most incredible thing he had to do, though he didn't realize he was doing it. So when success seems to overwhelm us, the things that really matter are relationships because relationships become our true success story.

Psalms 118:25, 1 Samuel 18:14, Proverbs 18:24, John 15:15

Review and Reflect
- Lifelong educator.
- Lifelong coach.
- Lifelong teacher.
- Lifelong administrator.
- Lifelong friend.

Quotable Quote

"The most meaningful success story is friendship."

Cycling Log

Bike/Type _____ Day _____ Month _____ Year _____

Weather: ☐ Sunny ☐ Cloudy ☐ Windy ☐ Rain ☐ Snow ☐ Other

Read: Topic of the day

_____

_____

Ride and Record

Miles _____ Route _____

Time _____ Average Speed _____

Revolt

Change, goals, thoughts of the day

_____

_____

_____

_____

_____

_____

- 31-day reading plan: Proverbs 25

Day 24 - Smile

O ne of the most important things you can do to improve your looks is to learn how to smile! More people will enjoy being around you when you smile. I didn't understand the impact of this when I was younger, but I did it all the time and people noticed. A lot of people would comment and call me smiley and so on and so forth.

When I was in my senior year in high school, I gave up all sports except for the one I really loved, basketball. We got a new coach and a new system of play, run and gun! It was fun and exciting to play and watch as we ran up the score clock nearly every night before the three-pointer[7] existed on our court. The whole time I was smiling because I was happy with life on and off the court. Even when the

---

[7] A three-point field goal is a field goal in a basketball game made from beyond the three-point line, a designated arc surrounding the basket. The three-pointer, as it is also called, was not adopted by the National Basketball Association until the 1979-1980 season.

other team was frustrated at our constant pursuit and attack, I kept smiling.

Once in a heated game, I was forced out of bounds on a short side court that had a short wall and rail. I caught myself as I fell into the rail and came back up immediately, smiling. My coach couldn't believe it. Anyone else would have come up ready for a confrontation. But for me it was just part of the game that I loved and enjoyed playing.

It wasn't until later years that I really discovered the power of what was going on. My nephew asked me about my high school coach, Coach Daniels. He was attending his camp at a local school when he began giving a speech about attitude and his first job as a high school head coach. It turns out that the speech was about me and the fact that I was always smiling.

Those were great days, and we had a great run in my senior year. When I think back to those days, all I see is my coach's smile. He reminds me that if we would have had the three-point line, we would have won the State Championship that year. It always brings back some great memories and reminds me of the lessons I learned that year.

I've turned the word smile into an acronym that stands for: Successfully Motivating, Inspiring Lives Every day! It is true that your smile has the power to inspire and will help your attitude for success. Today I continue to do my best to smile, and I have carried that throughout my life. Everywhere I have ever worked, people have made comments about my smile. The other thing is that everyone tells me how much I look like my mom. Needless to say, she always wears a smile, too.

There is nothing better than a good ride, and nothing seems to bring a bigger smile to my face than time spent in the saddle. Share the road and share a smile or two. You will be glad you did. Others will notice the countenance of the one who smiles often. Be careful not to open your mouth too wide, though. You might add some unexpected protein to your diet!

I can't help but believe the Lord is smiling as He looks down upon our lives and is ready to richly bless us. "The Lord bless you and keep you; the Lord make His face shine upon you and be gracious to you; the Lord turn His face toward you and give you peace." *Numbers 6:24-26 NIV*

Review and Reflect

• Smiling will improve your looks.
• Stay calm in the game.
• Your smile has the power to inspire.
• Share the road. Share a smile.

Quotable Quote

The success of your smile depends on your smile!"

Cycling Log

Bike/Type _____ Day _____ Month _____ Year _____

Weather: ☐ Sunny ☐ Cloudy ☐ Windy ☐ Rain ☐ Snow ☐ Other

Read: Topic of the day

_____

_____

Ride and Record

Miles _____ Route _____

Time _____ Average Speed _____

Revolt

Change, goals, thoughts of the day

_____

_____

_____

_____

_____

_____

• 31-day reading plan: Proverbs 26

Day 25 - The Four Seasons

W hen I refer to the four seasons, I am not talking about the music group of the 1960s, I am talking about the four seasons of the cyclist. Here I want to use the seasons we see in nature to cycle through the seasons that all of us go through in life. They are winter, spring, summer and fall. No one knows the importance of a season more than a farmer, and this is why Jesus in the Bible used the seasons to teach people, so they would gain understanding.

As I see it, in life we all go through seasons at different times, and how we view them and deal with them are very important to our success. One thing is for certain. Like the farmer, we cannot predict the weather. We just have to trust that we know what to do in each season. The same is true in life. We can never predict what circumstances we will face in our day-to-day. Each season of our life will bring its own challenges. Just like the farmer who depends on the rain for his crops, we too depend on a type of rain for our success.

For many of us, the toughest season is winter, especially in areas where winters tend to be long. Winter can bring harsh reality to us and leave us feeling very barren. But the truth of the matter is that beneath the dormant, dark stages things are happening. We simply have to pay attention to the signs. Winter is a season of rest, a season in which the soil is replenished, a season to reflect on what was and what will be. The real key is to look forward, as the next season is just around the corner.

Spring is probably everyone's favorite time of the year, unless of course you suffer from seasonal allergies. Spring is the time of new beginnings and possibilities. Training comes to mind. For the farmer, it is about planting and the expectation of the fall plantings emerging from the soil. It is truly an exciting time of year. Many of us begin planting gardens. There is nothing better than fresh produce from the garden.

Summer means everything to those school kids who are ready for a break. For the farmer, it is the season of growing, watching all the hard work grow and ripen from the seed that was planted. These are good times for everybody involved. We see so much opportunity in this season.

Before we know it, the season will change again to that melancholy time of year, fall. Following harvest, fall can be the most relaxing time of the year. It's a great time to celebrate the bounties of the summer! For the farmer, this is true as well. The days become shorter, and before you know it, preparation time is here again. Fall is a good time for reflection and looking ahead to improvements in advance of the next season.

It's amazing how much this all ties into cycling. Naturally and spiritually, we can easily see how the seasons relate to us. There are four things typically going on in our lives: sowing, reaping, resting and ripening. We all need to sow good works to produce good results. The Bible is clear on the subject of doing good and reaping what you sow. We have also covered resting in this book and how important it is. Ripening is the growing stage that we all go through at different stages of our lives, but it seems to never stop. And of course we enjoy the rewards of reaping a good harvest if we have done the work of preparation, sowing and tilling.

We can only do our part and expect the rest to come into play. I am referring to rain because that is the one thing that is out of our control. That is where trust comes in and we depend on the one true source of rain, God. He determines when to allow the rain to fall. He only asks that we have faith in Him. The scripture is clear: "He ... sends rain on the righteous and the unrighteous" (*Matthew 5:45*) and it is He who makes things grow.

So in the end, keep cycling. Keep going and don't give up. Don't quit. The rain will come in time, and days of refreshing will follow. The Bible makes it clear that there will always be a time to plant and a time to harvest, as long as the earth remains. So keep trusting and keep believing. Like a good farmer, don't stop doing what you know to do when it's right and good.

Ecclesiastes 3:1-14, Genesis 8:22, Matthew 5:45, 1 Corinthians 6-8, James 5:7

Review and Reflect
- Four Seasons
- Winter: Resting
- Spring: Sowing
- Summer: Ripening
- Fall: Reaping
- God = Rain

Quotable Quote

"Keep sowing, it's the only way you will avoid crop failure."

Cycling Log

Bike/Type _____ Day _____ Month _____ Year _____

Weather: ☐ Sunny ☐ Cloudy ☐ Windy ☐ Rain ☐ Snow ☐ Other

Read: Topic of the day

_____

_____

Ride and Record

Miles _____ Route _____

Time _____ Average Speed _____

Revolt

Change, goals, thoughts of the day

_____

_____

_____

_____

_____

_____

- 31-day reading plan: Proverbs 27

Day 26 - The Dream Cycle

The dream cycle goes back to something that I wrote earlier and that I'd like to repeat. To realize your dreams, you have to first say your dream out loud, then write it down, and then actively work on it. Start with a dream you have and write it down. Form a vision around it and then actively work on it. That is the only way I know our dreams can be realized and materialized. Any goal we have in life has to be fleshed out. It's just the way it works. Putting legs on your dreams is the only way to run with them. In this case putting wheels on our dreams is the only way to ride those dreams.

My mom loved creamsicles, those orange popsicles that had vanilla ice cream hidden in the middle. I called them dreamsicles! As a kid I wasn't crazy about the flavor, but as I grew older I acquired a taste for them. And even the cream soda flavored soda pop reminded me of them.

Sometimes dreams are filled with unexpected things, like vanilla ice cream, and we have to acquire a taste for these things. It's not a bad thing. We just have to realize that a lot goes into big dreams. Big dreams don't usually come on a stick, like corn dogs at the Texas

State Fair. They take work, faith and just good old-fashioned, roll up your sleeves elbow grease and a whole lot of no's before the yeses come alive.

Now that I'm approaching 50, it is becoming more and more clear that I haven't dreamed big enough to date. While I am writing this to you I also am looking to expand my dream horizons, dreams that I can ride away on. If I can't pack it, I don't want to back it. In other words, if the dream is only big enough for me to fulfill, it isn't a big enough dream. My dream needs to take others with it.

If you're a dreamer like me, you might have a pretty wild imagination. I know I do. As a kid, I remember a dream that was so vivid to me that I woke up believing it. The dream was about a purple mini bike my Dad had gotten for me and left in our garage. The next morning I was so excited, I wanted to rush down and see my new purple mini bike parked in the garage. I remember waking up and looking from the bedroom window, expecting to see the mini bike parked in front of the garage. I ran down the stairs immediately to go check out the "dream cycle," only to be very disappointed.

Dreams need wheels and the axis from which to drive from. Relationships are the same. They need a center axis from which to turn. How you relate to your dreams will determine how real they will become in your life. Build a relationship with your dreams that you can marry for life. Make them your companion as you ride along the trails and highways of life. Don't lose sight of what is important to you, and if it is purple, well that's the power of dreams.

Genesis 37:5

Review and Reflect

- Dreams need to be spoken.
- Dreams need to be written.
- Dreams need to be active.
- Dreams need an axis.
- Build a relationship with your dreams.

Quotable Quote

*"How you relate to your dreams will determine
how real your dreams become."*

Cycling Log

Bike/Type _____ Day _____ Month _____ Year _____

Weather: ☐ Sunny ☐ Cloudy ☐ Windy ☐ Rain ☐ Snow ☐ Other

Read: Topic of the day

_____

_____

Ride and Record

Miles _____ Route _____

Time _____ Average Speed _____

Revolt

Change, goals, thoughts of the day

_____

_____

_____

_____

_____

_____

- 31-day reading plan: Proverbs 28

Day 27 - Rewards

O ne of the greatest advantages of a revolution is the rewards that come with it. Though the battles are hard fought, they're all worth it in the end. Within those results are the many rewards for your hard work, and the result of the battle is that what needed to be changed did change.

Enjoying change is so refreshing you can't help but revel in it! The results can be life changing on many levels. No longer are you enslaved to what once dictated you. Freedom has become your biggest reward. Now you have options that were once not there.

Cycling can make you or break you, depending on how you approach it. The strategy here is to stay consistent with the five steps you have learned. Keep reading, keep riding, keep recording, keep revolting (as necessary) and keep repeating. This is how you build consistency in your life.

Consistency over speed will get you closer to your goals, and the success and the rewards that come with it will be better than anything else. Microwaved success won't last as long as well done, marinated ideas and strategies. With these come long-term benefits.

It's like taking delayed gratification over instant, like real potatoes over instant. Waiting generates the strength you need to give you the ability to pedal up the hills of difficulty when they come.

Everyone likes rewards, whether they are big or small. It is like being the first one to open up the box of cereal so you can get the prize! Do they still sell cereal with prizes? Anyway, the point is that rewards are important to us. That is why every credit card company offers us those incentives to get us to use their card. Rewards are a great motivator, and many times rewards have given me a reason to ride, like I really needed one.

The Bible even speaks about rewards. Our future hope relies on the rewards that Christ has promised us. Who wouldn't want a new and better home, continual feasting, rest and total peace along with a crown? These are just a few of the perks, if you will, offered to those who choose to believe and put their faith in the savior Jesus Christ. That is a pretty awesome deal, though I am not sure about wearing a crown. I will probably just leave the crown at the feet of our one true King, as He is the one who deserves to wear a crown!

Remember that along with rewards, comes that much needed rest. There is no struggle in rest. Rest is the place of relaxation. Take a deep breath and be thankful today that you have rest, even when it doesn't feel like it. The hammock of life is waiting for you in a gently shaded spot, with a refreshing drink and perhaps a good book like this, or just a much needed nap. Enjoy it, you deserve it!

Hebrews 11:6

Review and Reflect

- Revolutions bring rewards.
- Freedom means having choices.
- Rewards are good, big or small.
- Rest is a result of rewards.
- Enjoy it, you deserve it.

Quotable Quote

"The unseen rewards of life are some of the greatest!"

Cycling Log

Bike/Type _____ Day _____ Month _____ Year _____

Weather: ☐ Sunny ☐ Cloudy ☐ Windy ☐ Rain ☐ Snow ☐ Other

Read: Topic of the day

_____

_____

Ride and Record

Miles _____ Route _____

Time _____ Average Speed _____

Revolt

Change, goals, thoughts of the day

_____

_____

_____

_____

_____

_____

- 31-day reading plan: Proverbs 29

Day 28 - Finish

When it comes to professional sports, Oklahoma has the NBA team Oklahoma City Thunder. But for years, the University of Oklahoma (OU) football team was the closest thing we had to a professional team. In 2014, OU had high hopes, and polls showed that people were expecting their success. But as it went on, the season proved to become a dismal one.

Early that fall, I had a dream about meeting Oklahoma University football head coach Bob Stoops and Nick Saban[8] of Alabama. Why I was dreaming about two coaches I had never met is beyond me. It not only happened once, but twice. At that point I began to pay attention to what was happening throughout the season.

The dream went something like this: I was speaking to students and faculty at the University of Oklahoma about running and cycling. I am not a professor, except at night, in my dreams. After the speech, Bob Stoops came up to me and handed me a check and thanked me for my time and ministry. While I was recovering from the shock of Bob Stoops coming up to me, Nick Saban walked up,

---

[8]   Head coach of the Alabama Crimson Tide football team.

shook my hand, and handed me a much larger check! In my amazement, I woke up.

As the season progressed and many began to call for Bob Stoops to leave, I felt the need to pray for him. And so every day I prayed for a coach I had never met, a coach whose achievements I admired. I even prayed while I was riding my bike. After all, he was the most winning coach of all time at the University of Oklahoma and is one of the most winning active coaches of today. The records speak for themselves and I couldn't see any reasonable reason to make a change, even though Oklahoma had a less than average season of 8-5 and we had lost our bowl game.

Obviously, changes were made, and by the time the new season was starting, all eyes were on Big Game Bob[9]. Would there be an answer to all the questions surrounding his ability? Again, he proved to have the ability to put together another winning team, and he found himself in the new playoff system in 2015. Guess who was also right there? None other than Nick Saban and his football team, the Alabama Crimson Tide. By this time I was thinking could this really be happening?

If you watch any college football, you know the rest of the story. It was Nick Saban and the Alabama "Roll Tide" who once again emerged a winner. One word summed up their whole season: Finish. It was the mentality to finish every game, the mentality to leave it all on the field that led them to another National Championship. Congratulations Nick!

So the challenge before you is to finish the cycle that began when you opened this book. Finish strong and continue to finish every moment of every day until you reach your goal of success in your life.

---

[9] Bob Stoops earned this nickname for winning big games early in his coaching career.

Someday I hope to meet these two great coaches and shake their hands and tell them this story face to face. Those who have a successful mindset can adjust to adverse circumstances and turn things around.

You never know what dreams you may have or when our paths will cross. For now, my goal is to finish the cycle before me, this book! Although I may be finished here on this page, I believe this is only the beginning of something revolutionary!

2 Corinthians 8:11, Acts 20:24

Review and Reflect
- It started with a dream.
- Bob Stoops and Nick Saban.
- Dismal Oklahoma 2014 season.
- 2015 season turnaround.
- Finish.

Quotable Quote

"Finish what you start, it's the only way it will get done!"

Cycling Log

Bike/Type _____ Day _____ Month _____ Year _____

Weather: ☐ Sunny ☐ Cloudy ☐ Windy ☐ Rain ☐ Snow ☐ Other

Read: Topic of the day

_____

_____

Ride and Record

Miles _____ Route _____

Time _____ Average Speed _____

Revolt

Change, goals, thoughts of the day

_____

_____

_____

_____

_____

_____

- 31-day reading plan: Proverbs 30

Dedication

D edication is the engine that keeps you going when your motivation runs dry. You just keep doing what has to be done, whether you feel like it or not. The bottom line is commitment. Today, many lack this fundamental element in their lives. We all need help with our commitment. That is why it is so important for us to surround ourselves with people who will encourage us, motivate us and just be honest with us when we are falling short.

This is why I believe so much in dedicating our lives to God. Through His help and His direction we can achieve greater things. The Bible makes it clear that the church is a great place to surround yourself with people who will help you. If you haven't experienced that at a church you have visited, I apologize, but you need to find a different church. A true place of worship is dedicated to God and His people. That is what makes it alive. The relationship with Christ gives us a relationship with others and creates a family tie that is not easily broken. This is why the church has always been a great place.

I would like to dedicate this book to the many people who have been involved in forming my life over the past half century. They are, first and foremost, my parents, who brought me into a loving Christian home that included four siblings, three brothers and one sister. I was the youngest, so everything I learned came mostly from my family during my early years.

I would like to thank my church family over the years. This family includes several different churches that I have been involved with. There have been many good memories and life lessons I have learned along the way. Thankfully, my entire family shared in the experiences that shaped my vision of the church.

Friends are those few who I have always loved and appreciated for never changing. Our hair might be thinner and grey, but along with all the other signs of aging, we are showing signs of having lived a good life! There is no doubt my life would not be the same without you all.

Each year I encounter new people. Since I started writing this book, new acquaintances have become a part of my life, and I am enjoying getting to know them.

There is no doubt in my mind that I would not have written this book if it had not been for my loving wife and beautiful daughter. They inspire me to be the best husband and father that I can be. Hopefully they see me becoming the man God intended me to become.

Finally, and most importantly, I want to dedicate this book to my Lord and Savior Jesus Christ, who has given me the breath to breathe, this life to live and everything I have in it. Because of Him, I write to you, the reader, who I may encounter someday along the road of life. If I don't encounter you, I want you to know God's great love for you. It is truly He who will do the greatest work in you to revolutionize your life through His grace! I pray today that you will dedicate your life to Him, the one true God. His revolution is designed to turn your life around!

Cycling Log

Bike/Type _____ Day _____ Month _____ Year _____

Weather: ☐ Sunny ☐ Cloudy ☐ Windy ☐ Rain ☐ Snow ☐ Other

Read: Topic of the day

_____

_____

Ride and Record

Miles _____ Route _____

Time _____ Average Speed _____

Revolt

Change, goals, thoughts of the day

_____

_____

_____

_____

_____

_____

- 31-day reading plan: Proverbs 31

The Cyclist Creed

I believe, therefore I ride,
I believe in the age old words of the apostle's creed,
I believe in that message as the faith I need,
It's said 'what's good for the body is good for the soul'
But cycling alone cannot make me whole.
I need a savior and I need a friend,
To brace against life's weathering wind,
To ride with me along life's road,
To give me courage and make me bold.
I need 'the one' who calmed the sea,
Who makes the lame to walk and blind to see!
From this truth I cannot hide,
I believe, therefore I ride.
For the weak and poor and those in need,
I raise the banner of the cyclist creed,
Unspoken words are heard through action,
So give them voice and ride with passion!
Spoken truth needs to be heard,
Share the road and spread the word,
Son of God I have not denied,
I believe, therefore I ride!

By Jon Tucker
January 11, 2015

Resources

Here are just a few great resources for you to enjoy!

- 30 Years of building the body through cycling!
- www.thenationalbikechallenge.org - Join in the challenge that inspired me!
- www.thrive15.com - Help your business mind grow!
- www.influencers.org - Experience the journey!

About the Author

J on Tucker was born in Tulsa, Oklahoma on April 6, 1966 and was raised in Haskell, Oklahoma, where he resides today with his wife, Brenda, and their daughter, Gabrielle. He is currently employed as shift leader in the paper industry by Kimberly-Clark Corporation in Jenks, Oklahoma. His wife is a lifelong teacher and coach, while their daughter plays basketball under her mom and maintains high academic standards.

This is Jon's second book. He hopes to write more and encourage and influence people all over the world. To find out more visit the website.

www.cyclistinyou.com

Please feel free to email me at jon@cyclistinyou.com. I would love to hear your stories about Revolutions and how it has affected you!

Thanks for taking the time to read this book. I hope and pray it has helped you in some way. Remember, "if you are not cycling you are not living!"

CPSIA information can be obtained
at www.ICGtesting.com
Printed in the USA
LVOW12s1952290716

498127LV00008B/12/P